SEEING JESUS

Glimpses of God in My Life

Kim V. Engelmann

Foreword by James W. Moore

DIMENSIONS
FOR LIVING
NASHVILLE

D1228041

Library of Congress Cataloging-in-Publication Data

Engelmann, Kim.
   Seeing Jesus : glimpses of God in my life / Kim V. Engelmann.
     p. cm.
   Includes bibliographical references.
   ISBN 0-687-34182-5 (alk. paper)
   1. Christian life—Presbyterian authors.   I. Title.
   BV4501.3.E54 2004
   248.4′851—dc22

                                    2004015375

04 05 06 07 08 09 10 11 12 13–10 9 8 7 6 5 4 3 2 1

MANUFACTURED IN THE UNITED STATES OF AMERICA

Contents

Acknowledgments   5

Foreword by Dr. James W. Moore   7

Introduction   9

Chapter 1: Seeing Jesus by Expanding Your Context   11

Chapter 2: Seeing Jesus by Letting Go of What We Cling To   19

Chapter 3: Seeing Jesus in the Unexpected   27

Chapter 4: Seeing Jesus When He Seems Far Away   35

Chapter 5: Seeing Jesus in the Storms   43

Chapter 6: Seeing Jesus in the Mustard Seeds   53

Chapter 7: Seeing Jesus When You Are "Out on a Limb"   61

Chapter 8: Seeing Jesus in the Master Fiddler   69

Chapter 9: Seeing Jesus in Suffering   79

Notes   87

Acknowledgments

This book is a compilation of effort on the part of many. I wish to thank certain members of the pastoral staff at Menlo Park Presbyterian Church for their helpful critique and counsel on all of these chapters, which were formerly sermons. Most especially, my thanks to Doug Ferguson, John Ortberg, Doug Lawrence, Joanie Tankersley, Frank VanderZwan, and, early on, Scott Dudley. Finally, I'd like to thank Walt Gerber, who kept me on task with the persistent words, "What is it you want to say? Then, just say it!"

Thanks also to Nancy Florence, my administrative assistant, who put all of this in presentable, publishable form and kept encouraging me. Thanks to Mary Goerz for her wisdom and wonderful prayers. To my dear friends, Beth and Marie Frykberg, thank you for standing by me when I was sure all was lost and for pushing me to take leaps of faith that seemed unmanageable, but actually made me grow. Thanks to S.B. for the gleam of approval, for empathy, for unearthing treasure buried in pain—all of which made the impetus for this book possible.

Thanks to my loving family; to my three children, Christopher, Julie, and Jonathan, who "let Mommy write" without too much complaint and always made it possible for me to feel needed beyond what I could imagine; and to my dear husband, Tim, who continues to bring me coffee, wonderful companionship, and a love for life that is exhilarating and inspiring.

Foreword

"We meet you, O Christ, in many a guise; your image we see in simple and wise." These words from the gospel hymn pose a powerful and very personal issue that we would all do well to grapple with and consider: What does it mean to "see Jesus"? This is precisely what Kim Engelmann encourages and helps us do in this thoughtful and well-written book.

To put it in capsulated form, there are three kinds of vision:

- physical vision: seeing with our eyes,
- intellectual vision: seeing with our minds, and
- spiritual vision: seeing with our hearts and souls.

The miracles of God are all around us, but can we see them? People to help, opportunities to serve, and lessons to learn are all around us, but do we see them? The redemptive activities of Jesus Christ are happening all around us, but do we notice? Do we take them in? Can we really see them with our eyes, our minds, our hearts? Dr. Engelmann encourages us to "open our eyes" and see the presence of Jesus. It's the same notion that we see in the minds of some of our hymn writers. One wrote these words: "Open my eyes, that I may see glimpses of truth thou hast for me." And another wrote: "Turn your eyes upon Jesus. Look full in his wonderful face."

Our problem is that we rush through life at such a frantic pace that we shut down our spiritual sensitivities and don't take the time to look and really see. Though we have eyes, sadly sometimes we do not see.

For example, look at page 39 in this book. There, you will see a fascinating picture. At first glance, it may look to you like some blobs of ink splashed on a piece of paper, but if you refocus and look carefully you can suddenly see the face of Christ. Through this dramatic demonstration, Dr. Engelmann reminds us "how close our Lord is and ... how we can miss seeing him altogether in the midst of the clutter and terminal busyness of our days." But if we focus on Christ, every day will become a day of joy and confidence for us when we see Jesus in the center of it all.

That is what this book is about, and as we read it, our prayer could well be:

> Open my eyes, that I may see
> Glimpses of truth thou hast for me;
> Place in my hands the wonderful key
> That shall unclasp and set me free.
> Silently now I wait for thee,
> Ready, my God, thy will to see.
> Open my eyes, illumine me,
> Spirit divine.

Dr. James W. Moore

Introduction

his book is an outgrowth of a series of sermons given at Menlo Park Presbyterian Church and has been a joy to put together. It has amazed me throughout my ministry that I haven't yet run out of things to say. After graduating from seminary, one of my biggest concerns was that my well would soon dry up, all the Bible stories would be told, and then I would have to hang my hat and go elsewhere. Twenty years later, I feel that I have barely scratched the surface. I have learned over the years to trust the generative nature of scripture, its living relevancy and richness for people, and the way in which God uses scripture to transform broken lives.

This is a book about "seeing Jesus." At the end of the book of Job, Job is finally granted a vision of God, which causes him to declare, "Surely I spoke of things I did not understand, things too wonderful for me to know.... My ears had heard of you but now my eyes have seen you" (Job 42:3, 5). The truth expressed by these verses has been my guidepost both professionally and personally. Being raised in an academic environment, in which things were understood primarily in a linear fashion, I gradually discovered that such understanding, although helpful in a lot of ways, does not bring the kind of awareness of God's presence that Job had when he saw the Lord. The *experience* of Jesus is what catches you off guard, broadens and deepens your linear notions of what you think you understand by throwing you into a love relationship with God that is deeper and more fulfilling than any linear theory could ever be.

My prayer is that in the pages of this book you will not simply read *about* the One we worship. My prayer is rather that you would experience seeing the One who has known you and loved you before you were born. So if any of these words bring a little clarity of vision to that awesome One who loves beyond what we could ask or think, if any of these words help open spiritual eyes a little wider to the experience of grace, to the longing of God's heart to be in relationship with us, then it was well worth writing them down.

Chapter 1
Seeing Jesus by Expanding Your Context
"On Beyond Zebra"

Matthew 5:13-16, 38-44

I am the mother of three, and we love to read books together as a family. One of my favorite children's authors is also a theologian—the late Dr. Seuss, Theodore Geisel. Of course, he's not really a theologian, but I find theological meaning in his work. He wrote such books as *The Cat in the Hat, Horton Hears a Who,* and *Green Eggs and Ham.*[1] I think that one of his lesser known books, *On Beyond Zebra,* is one of his best. It's all about the serious problem that occurs when you stay within the limits of the twenty-six letters of the alphabet.

Conrad Cornelius O'Donnell O'Dell is the character in the book who is learning to spell. He begins in a very pedantic way, declaring, "A is for Apple" and "B is for Bear." After Conrad reaches "Z is for

Zebra," he thinks he is done. But his friend who is listening takes up a piece of chalk to draw one letter more. That letter is YUZZ, which he tells Conrad is the letter used to spell "Yuzz-a-ma-Tuzz." The story continues in classic Seuss style, introducing new letters that stand for completely fantastical things. The teacher tells Conrad that in the places he goes and the things that he sees, he could never survive if he stopped at the letter Z. Seuss continues:

> So, on beyond Z! It's high time you were shown
> That you really *don't* know all there is to be known.

And the book goes on with all kinds of fascinating letters and concepts that are beyond the ordinary, bringing in a whole new dimension by extending our normal conceptual frame of reference. Of course, this is child's play. *What can possibly be beyond Z?* you might ask! Z is as far as the alphabet goes, right? Once you've reached Z, you've reached the end. There is no more.

There are also times in our lives when it may seem that we've come to a halt. You might be at the end of the road in your life. It may feel that there are no more options, that life has dealt you a dead-end hand, and that you can never get beyond the Z. Maybe the end of the road for you is a divorce, the death of a loved one, financial ruin, or a serious medical illness. Or perhaps you've felt trapped in the doldrums, in the A to Z of routine; where it appears that there is no purpose to your life; and you are caught in the alphabet soup of the same old thing.

Seeing Jesus' Love in the Alphabet Soup of Life

If this is just another year of the same old A to Z, of nothing new, or if you think you are at the end of the road because of some pain in your life, be encouraged! These are exactly the times when Jesus Christ loves to take up the chalk of our lives—no matter how blunt and worn down—and draw one letter more. Perhaps even a letter we'd never dreamed of before.

I am using *On Beyond Zebra* as a metaphor to describe the awesome reality of the love of Jesus Christ for us that is "beyond Z," because it is more wonderful than we can conceive of in our normal A to Z frame of reference. The writer of Ephesians prays that we would experience or "know the love of Christ that surpasses knowledge" (3:19 NRSV). God's love creates new possibilities for us, bringing with it the seasoning of joy, expectancy, and hope.

Amazingly, these new possibilities come to us right where we are. In *On Beyond Zebra,* new letters are created using the existing twenty-six letters of the alphabet—such as the letter called Yuzz, spelled Y-U-Z-Z. In the same way, the "on beyond zebra" love of Jesus Christ uses the very situations we are in, meets us right where we are, and gives us a new purpose and hope, either by reconfiguring our circumstances or by changing our perspective.

My father died suddenly and unexpectedly—a massive stroke took his life as he went to the bank one Monday morning. I stood in the reception line after his memorial service for several hours listening to stories about how he had made a difference in people's lives and had so deepened their love for Jesus that ministry had new meaning for them.

My father was a professor at Princeton Seminary and had been trained at Harvard Divinity School. He was an academic, not prone to tears and emotion, ready to psychoanalyze a religious experience away in his earlier years. But none of this came up at the memorial service. What people mentioned was how much he loved Jesus and how a car accident changed his life.

This life-altering accident happened when I was a teenager, on the first day of a family vacation. We stopped to help two women with a flat tire. They stood on the shoulder of the New York thruway, waving a little white glove. We had parked in front of their disabled vehicle because we almost passed them. My father got out and was squatting down to change the tire when a man who had fallen asleep at the wheel while going sixty-five miles an hour smashed into the back of the car my father was working on. The car rolled over my father, grinding him along in the gravel until it slammed into the back of our parked camper. When my father struggled out from under the car, still conscious, he was torn up from stem to stern. He lay there for half an hour before anyone realized that no one had called an ambulance.

At the hospital, almost an hour and a half later, the doctor said he wasn't sure my father would live. He was turning blue, his lung was bleeding, and they needed to get him on oxygen as soon as they could. First, however, he needed quick surgery. As he was being wheeled into surgery, he felt this "on beyond zebra" love, this palpable presence of Jesus, pouring into him. He began to sing "Fairest Lord Jesus"—an old familiar hymn—to the masked, somber surgical staff. The nurse poked him and told him, "You can't sing that. The doctor is Jewish." "Okay," said my father, "let's discuss the Old Testament." They did, and as they did, my father turned from blue to pink, his lung stopped bleeding, and the oxygen was cancelled.

This "on beyond zebra" encounter with the healing love of God forever changed my father's approach to theology. His head knowledge frame of reference was seasoned with heart knowledge, and when he returned to Princeton, he began doing things a different way. He became known as the weeping professor, for whenever he mentioned the name of Jesus during a lecture, tears often welled up in his eyes. He never stopped being an intellectual, but now his lectures were also filled with heart knowledge as well. His great love for Jesus was what people remembered at his memorial service. And by his person, he taught me to love Jesus as well.

One of my favorite scriptures comes from the book of Job. After Job has lost everything and has a long intellectual debate with his friends about it, God appears on the scene: "I spoke of things . . . too wonderful for me to know," says Job to God. "My ears had heard of you but now my eyes have seen you" (Job 42:3, 5).

That personal encounter with God changed everything for Job. Knowing *about* God was nothing compared to knowing God personally; his head knowledge was seasoned with heart knowledge. And in the last scene, God takes up the chalk and draws one letter more, restoring Job's fortunes entirely.

Jesus came to show us that this is what God is like. In the Beatitudes (Matthew 5), he essentially rewrites the Mosaic law, fulfilling it based on God's nature—"on beyond zebra" love. Notice what Jesus does in the words we read in Matthew 5. There's a repetition of the phrase over and over: "You have heard that it was said. . . . But I say to you" that there's another way. Conventional wisdom and practice tells you to "love your neighbors and hate your enemies"—this is the way it has always been done in the normal A to Z world—but Jesus turns this upside down, telling us instead to "love your enemies." You have heard that it was said, "An eye for an eye and a tooth for a tooth." This is the status quo, the A to Z way. But I say to you, "If anyone strikes you on the right cheek, turn the other also." Jesus ushered in this new order, this New-Testament-On-Beyond-Zebra way of being in the world and loving the world. Once we are touched by God's "on beyond zebra" love in Jesus Christ, we are called to do things in a different way, to become the salt of the earth.

In all the churches I served, we had potlucks, but I have never really liked them. By the time you get a bite of every casserole on your plate so you don't hurt anyone's feelings, not only does the plate buckle, but also everything also ends up tasting bland and alike for some reason. I used salt—a lot of salt!—and it helped. A little shake from the outside brought the entire mound of casseroles to life. I understand why people leave the church. Religion without the salty experience of God's "on beyond zebra" love is bland, boring, and irrelevant. Knowing the love of Jesus personally ushers in a whole new way of being in the world, a salty way, a zesty way. The reality of Jesus' love becomes our passion and redefines everything we do.

A car accident could have been the end of my father's life. Instead, God broke in and seasoned it, transforming it for his purposes. What's the worst thing that's ever happened to you? Is it something so painful that you wonder whether you'll ever get beyond it? Give it over to the One who is a Master at making a way, "on beyond zebra," taking the chalk and drawing one letter more, when the rest of the world tells you there is no way through or around your situation.

I was recently told about a painting. Evidently it depicts two people playing chess. The positions of the pieces on the board seem to indicate to the observer of the painting that the chess game is over. That one player is in checkmate. But one day a master chess player saw the painting and after studying it declared, "The painting is wrong. The king is not in checkmate. He has one more move." And as the story goes, the master chess player was right. God has one more move for you. Something you view as a sunset may actually be a sunrise in the context of God's "on beyond zebra" love for you. Remember:

- Your life matters to God—it is valuable and counts!
- God loves you with "on beyond zebra" love—a love that surpasses our A-Z knowledge, a love that never gives up on you, a love that knows you better than you know yourself.
- No matter what the situation, you will never find yourself at the end (at Z) with no options if you belong to Jesus Christ. God always has one more move for you—a new letter to draw with the chalk of your life.

And once you believe that you are loved that much, then you will have something salty to share with the world!

Questions for Reflection

1. Can you remember a time when it felt as if there was no way out, and God made a way for you? What were the circumstances?

2. Are there situations that you have stopped praying about because it seems that there is no hope? How might you regain hope in the transforming power of Jesus Christ?

3. What are the most meaningful scriptures, experiences, and thoughts that have helped you be aware of God's ability to take the most difficult situations and use them for good?

4. Would knowing that God's love is deeper than anything bad that could ever happen to us affect the way you live each day? How so?

SEEING JESUS

Dear Lord Jesus, You always make a way where there seems to be no way. Your presence transformed the cross into resurrection, and I know your presence can transform whatever cross I am carrying today. I trust you to do this, and I leave the baggage of my circumstances in your hand, knowing that no matter how difficult I find this journey of life, you are with me to renew me, strengthen me, and work all things for good. In Jesus' name I pray. Amen.

Chapter 2

Seeing Jesus by Letting Go
of What We Cling To

"With Open Hands"

2 Corinthians 12:9; Galatians 2:20; John 20:21-22

Lord, make me an instrument of your peace. Where there is hatred, let me sow love. Where there is injury, pardon. Where there is doubt, faith. Where there is despair, hope. Where there is darkness, light, and where there is sadness, joy. O Divine Master, grant that I may not so much seek to be consoled, as to console. To be understood, as to understand. To be loved, as to love. For it is in giving, that we receive; it is in pardoning that we are pardoned; and it is in dying, that we are born to eternal life. Amen.[1]

The prayer of Saint Francis of Assisi is one of the most famous of all Christian writings. It asks God to give us the power to do what is not humanly possible—to replace hatred with love, doubt with faith, sadness with joy. In essence, the prayer asks God to give us the power to change ourselves and change the world for Jesus

Christ. Yet, this prayer may seem too idealistic for us who do not live in cloisters or monasteries; we who have schedules, demands, and ongoing obligations.

Recently I opened up a checking account at a nearby bank. This bank's motto, written in huge black letters on the window, was "You Have More Power Than You Think."[2] I couldn't help admiring the motto. I could see how it would be a tremendous draw in times like today when we feel powerless about what is going on around us. Who knows? Maybe a checking account at this particular bank was the answer to it all! And yet, I began to think about the difference between power as our culture defines it and power as Christians define it, and how easy it is to slip into substituting our cultural definition of power for world-changing Holy Spirit power.

If I curl my hand into a tight fist, this represents power the way our culture defines it. Study the fist position carefully sometime. Ask yourself what a hand can do when it is in this position. If nothing else, it certainly can pack a wallop, can't it? When I went to college in Manhattan, New York, I took a self-defense class and learned how to pack some power behind an arm thrust and a fist.

A hand in the shape of a fist is also much smaller than an open hand. Sometimes when we try very hard to win battles or gain points in order to be more powerful as the world defines power, ironically our world becomes constricted, just like a fist. Our perspective grows smaller, our world becomes no bigger than the problem at hand, our solutions are forged with tension, and we feel as though any resolution to a problem is all up to us. Have you ever felt that way? I certainly have. But the worst part about it is that this kind of power quest—and we might even define power here as the need to control—affects those closest to me whom I love the most: my family and friends. I can't hold anyone else's hand when my fingers are rolled up underneath my thumb. Making a fist is a solitary stance. I can't give anything or receive anything either; and giving and receiving is the living dynamic of any relationship. Isn't it odd that a clenched fist, so impractical and ineffective, is considered threatening and powerful?

When you release your fist, slowly and carefully, you can feel tension leaving your hand. Opening your hand, palm upward to the sky, is a far more vulnerable position. But your fingers are able to touch and reach and stretch in freedom. You are now able to hold things, to offer things, to receive things. It feels much better this way, and so much more can be accomplished. An open hand is better equipped to do what it was created to do.

A quote making the rounds these days is, "Do not feel totally, personally, irrevocably responsible for everything. That's my job. Hand it over. (Signed,) God." When we open our hands and relinquish our control, we actually do have more power than we think, though it has nothing to do with higher interest rates, free checking, or yield on investments as the bank might define it.

It has to do with the Lord's statement to Paul when he says, "My grace is sufficient for you, for power is made perfect in weakness" (2 Corinthians 12:9 NRSV). Weakness and power together—that's the catch. It's literally hard to grasp because weakness and power don't usually fit hand in glove. But the scriptures are full of such paradoxical truth, turning the world's values and expectations upside down and inside out.

Paul says again, "I have been crucified with Christ and I no longer live, but Christ lives in me" (Galatians 2:20). And this truth is so deeply embedded in the event of Christ crucified in weakness that once you discover that your weakness is actually a venue for his strength, you are onto what Jesus meant when he said, "Whoever finds his life will lose it, and whoever loses his life for my sake will find it" (Matthew 10:39). It's the paradox understood and echoed by Saint Francis of Assisi who wrote that "it is in giving that we receive." In our vulnerability, in the emptying of ourselves, his strength in us finds a home.

I came out to California six years ago as a single parent of a four-month-old, a two-year-old, and a four-year-old. Well-meaning individuals told me that my marriage of fifteen years was over and that I needed to move on. I was alone except for the one friend who had invited me to come to California. Until then, I had always been able to handle things. But on my own, I couldn't seem to muster enough strength to keep going. The days were long and lonely. I wanted the phone to ring, but it didn't. I wanted someone to invite me over, but no one knew me. At night I'd fall into bed exhausted, wondering why I was alive and how on earth I could possibly make it through the next day. I'm terribly stubborn when it comes to admitting that I can't handle things, can't hang on by myself, and can't make it on my own. But I was forced, purely by a need to survive, to open my clenched fist that had been tightly locked for so long trying to keep my little world together. I had to surrender my efforts and ask for help. "Lord," I whispered, "I don't know what the future holds, and I don't know why you let this happen to me. I can't go another day on my own. Meet me in my weakness with your power, and change my world."

It hurt to open up. My muscles had been tightly clenched for so long. But as I reached out in weakness, I was met by the tremendous power of God's grace, both directly in prayer and through other Christians. And there is no greater power, no greater love. When you stand in the presence of Almighty God, knowing how vulnerable you really are, and open your hands to surrender and receive, God is there with more than enough. Things were still difficult, the days were still long, and I was still tired. But in my attempt to surrender, I think I let go just enough that God had some breathing room. Little miracles began to happen, and God's grace became more apparent like a gentle rhythm being played under the hum of daily activity: a part-time job with flexible hours dropped in my lap, a wonderful baby-sitter suddenly became available, my kindergartner somehow got into the class with the teacher whom everyone wanted, and people's love began to invade our lives. A year and a half later, the biggest miracle of all occurred: my marriage was restored and has grown and deepened into something better than it had ever been before.

I tell you this story so that you can know that whatever life circumstance you are up against, no matter what the pain or the difficulty, your job as a beloved child of God is simply to open your hands and give it to God. When we have done all that we can do, when we have tried all that we can try, when the tension in our fists begins to ache and it seems as if we are merely pummeling the air, Jesus meets us and says, "Open your hands so that I can grasp them and lead the way."

But this call to open your hands is not a call to complacency. It is not a call to resignation or to abandon our mission and desire to do what is right. Instead, we are called to surrender our agenda for God's agenda; and as we receive God's grace, we are compelled to give it away again. After a while, the very act of giving actually becomes a means of grace to receive. Paradoxically, in our surrender, we find the abundant life we long for. With open hands to give, we receive. This stance is what actually empowers us to follow Jesus, as his strength is made perfect in our weakness. In his 1980 Nobel Peace Prize acceptance speech, Adolfo Pérez Esquivel said:

> Because of [our] faith in Christ and humankind, we must apply our humble efforts [to the construction of] a more just and humane world.... To create this new society we must reach out our hands, fraternally, without hatred and rancour, for reconciliation and peace, with unfaltering determination in the defense of truth and justice. We know we cannot plant seeds with closed fists. To sow we must open our hands.[3]

Jesus was not crucified with a clenched fist. He gave up his agenda for God's agenda when he prayed, "Not my will, but yours be done." He reaches out to us with hands painfully open. We see the wounds there, and we might tend to doubt the effectiveness of such a stance. But the words of Jesus to Thomas on the day that he appeared resurrected with the scars still visible were these: "Peace be with you. As the Father has sent me, so I send you.... Receive the Holy Spirit" (John 20:21-22 NRSV).

So go out into the world with open hands to make a difference, letting go of your agenda and receiving the agenda of the Holy Spirit, which is much more power than you think. You will need the power of the Holy Spirit because it isn't the world's way to be open and vulnerable and willing to sacrifice. It's a hard thing to do to keep your hands open, but it is the only way to love as God loves. And it is the only way to bring change that lasts.

Mark, a family friend who graduated from Princeton Theological Seminary, went back to his country, Africa, to minister. He was in an impoverished area and had a small struggling church that he loved. As he was ministering there, teaching the people about the love of Jesus, he also began to empower them to make a difference in their community. The government grew fearful of the Christians and sent armed men to kill Mark. The men overpowered him and brutalized him with repeated stabbings. As this young pastor struggled for his life, he kept crying out to them, "Jesus loves you. I forgive you. You are better than this." And although they had been told to kill him, they left him alive, though barely. One of the attackers told him later that he couldn't bring himself to kill Mark when he told them that he forgave him in the midst of his torment. Mark was in the hospital for a long time. The church rallied around him, and in the wake of this disaster, this tiny impoverished church raised enough money to pay for every single one of Mark's hospital bills. The stance of the church was so strong that the government formally apologized to Mark. Because of Mark's vulnerability, his willingness to forgive, and his openhanded willingness to continue his ministry after that incident, the church grew and thrived under his leadership.

"His strength made perfect in our weakness." God is able to act with more power than we think when we become vulnerable and give up our own power struggle for control, advancement, success, or social status. When we relinquish our fear of the future or of whatever keeps our fists clenched, the power of the love of God in our midst can have free rein and can change the world through us.

You may be thinking, "How can I change the world? I can't even think about that. My life is so wretched, and I'm in such pain. I don't even know how to trust God enough to open up." Let me

25

encourage you to try to open your hands, just a little, because changing the world out there begins with change on the inside. God can handle whatever is keeping your fists clenched, and once you let go, God will be able to move in wonderful ways in your life with more power than you ever thought possible.

As we give up our white-knuckled agenda for God's agenda—shown to us by a living, powerful Savior who was crucified for us with open hands—we find Jesus. We see Jesus, and his strength is made perfect in our weakness.

Questions for Reflection

1. What situations cause you to constrict spiritually into a fist? When you are postured in this way, what is most helpful in allowing you to open up?

2. How can we live life in an open and receptive way, rather than in a strident and rigid way? What scripture helps with this principle?

3. What have you experienced that allows you to understand the value of open hands?

4. What does learning to open up mean in practical terms for your life at home, in your business, and in friendships?

Dear Jesus, at times I have wanted to hold on so tightly that I have stifled your life within me. I have been afraid to let go. Help me trust you more and rest in your amazing grace, so that I can live life with hands open for giving and receiving. In Jesus' name, I pray. Amen.

Chapter 3

Seeing Jesus in the Unexpected

"Expecting God's Surprises"

Matthew 7:11; Philippians 4:19; Hebrews 12:2

One day our hamster, Nugget, got out of his cage, and we couldn't find him. My eight-year-old daughter, Julie, prayed for Nugget's safe return and actually expected the Lord to cause her hamster to reappear at any moment, alive, unharmed, and in his right mind. She had no doubt. Now, it's not that I didn't believe that God could rescue a hamster at large, but I could certainly think of many better things that God could be doing. By the fourth night, I had a well-rehearsed speech prepared for Julie that included Nugget frolicking in the sunflower seed fields of heaven with other hamsters just his age. But for reasons only a mom would know, I couldn't bring myself to say anything. On the sixth night of Julie's hamster prayer vigil, Nugget came running back into the house through a screen door that had somehow been left ajar—in spite of all the skunks, raccoons, cats, and badgers our backyard harbors. He was half the size he had been upon departure but otherwise seemed completely fine. My daughter was pleased, but since she had been expecting this to happen all along, she was not nearly as ecstatic as I was. "I knew God would bring Nugget back," she said nonchalantly as she plopped him in his cage and went to bed.

I shared this story with someone just recently and he said, "Yeah, we prayed for our hamster, too, but never saw him again." Clearly prayers are not always answered in a predictable, formulaic sort of way. There are a lot of things that get in the way of prayer and a lot of things that we don't understand about how God works in our lives—especially in regard to hamsters. However, my daughter's rigorous expectancy reminded me that very often when I pray, I don't necessarily expect anything out of the ordinary to occur at all. I forget that as soon as a prayer is on my lips, God begins to act on my behalf—that's simply God's promise to us. Jesus said: "If you, then, though you are evil, know how to give good gifts to your children, how much more will your Father in heaven give good gifts to those who ask him!" (Matthew 7:11).

The answer to our prayer might not happen exactly the way we wish or occur precisely when we think it should, but this promise of Jesus is a call to expectation. Scripture challenges us to look forward, sit on the edge of our seat, and be poised and ready to celebrate what God will do next in our lives.

I am greatly comforted by this promise in Matthew. Maybe it's because misery loves company, but I am reminded that the early Christians must have experienced the difficulties and struggles that I do. Surely they also sometimes harbored low expectations about what God can and will do for us.

The early Christians certainly had reasons for their low expectations. Look at the backdrop of the story of Peter in Acts. It's heart-wrenching. James, the brother of John, has just been put to death by Herod. Others in the church have been seized and are being persecuted. This was a discouraging, fearful, uncertain time for Christians. I don't know why Peter was rescued but James put to death. What I do know is that our Lord was very aware that his people needed a burst of encouragement; they needed to be reminded that God was more powerful and more active on their behalf than they could ever fathom even though the circumstances seemed to dictate otherwise.

I love the way Luke writes, "So Peter was kept in prison *but...*" But what? Peter sat in a dark ominous prison tower, chained to Herod's soldiers with four squads of guards watching him, and awaited trial the next morning. Sounds pretty dismal, doesn't it? There doesn't seem to be any conditional clause. "But," writes Luke, "the church was earnestly praying to God for him." Oh yes, we may think, how nice. What a supportive gesture. Clearly the early Christians believed in the power of prayer. Clearly they knew the seriousness of Peter's situation. But what was their expectation level on a scale of one to ten—one being nothing and ten being ready for anything? Let's get the rest of the story.

Luke tells us that as they were praying for Peter, they heard knocking at the door. They must have wondered who on earth would be calling so late at night. They summoned Rhoda, the servant girl, and sent her to answer the door because they were busy praying for Peter.

And they continued their prayers: "O Lord, we don't understand why this has happened but please bring glory to your name through this. Save Peter and rescue him" (my paraphrase).

Suddenly Rhoda was in the midst of the prayer meeting. "Uh, excuse me," she stammered, "I am very sorry to bother you, but Peter is standing outside." They told her, "You're nuts. It can't be. Peter is bound with chains, sleeping between two soldiers. Herod has four squads of four soldiers each watching him. Impossible!"

Then it came again: thump, thump, thump! Peter continued to knock because Rhoda hadn't thought to let him in and he was stuck outside, no doubt worried that soldiers might be pursuing and discover him.

I imagine that God was enjoying a chuckle at this point. It seems we belong to a God who just loves to do the unexpected—to break out of the frame of reference, the predictable box we have created for God and declare, with parental delight, "Surprise!"

Thump, thump, thump! Of course those ardent pray-ers of the early church still had difficulty believing that their prayers could have been answered that night. As we've said, the chips were down. They had endured a lot of difficulties and losses, and they were gearing themselves up for yet another. In spite of the evidence to the contrary, they concluded that Peter was dead and that his ghost was haunting their premises. Throughout their discussion, Peter kept knocking. Finally, in a frightened little huddle, they swung open the door. When they saw their beloved fisherman standing before them, they were so astonished and made such a racket that Peter had to tell them to quiet down. "Shhh!" he tells them, "let me tell you what the Lord has done for me."

Thank goodness, God does wonderful things in spite of our meager outlook on the future. It was just as hard to believe good news in first-century Christianity as it is to believe now, even when the reality of answered prayer pounds at the door of our hearts, calling us to believe the good news that God is on our side and that the Lord is doing a new thing: "And my God will meet all your needs according to his glorious riches in Christ Jesus" (Philippians 4:19).

Our human nature tends to cause us to believe the worst. What if it's not true? What if it's true for everyone except for me? What if God really isn't doing much of anything these days, anyway?

These doubts come from past disappointments. Life hurts and things don't always work out the way we might want. What we pray for doesn't always occur the way we think it should, and that can be discouraging. But just because things don't happen the way we think they should happen does not mean that God is not acting on our behalf. God in Jesus Christ can be trusted to bring us through the trials of the cross to resurrection every time. Because of Jesus' faith and expectation that God was bigger than the cross, Jesus was able to endure the cross. Hebrews 12:2 tells us, "Let us fix our eyes on Jesus, the author and perfecter of our faith, who for the joy set before him endured the cross . . . and sat down at the right hand of the throne of God."

God is very good at bringing victory out of suffering—completely trustworthy in any circumstance. And once we trust in God's ability to bring resurrection out of even the worst situation or evil deed, we can wait expectantly for the *thump, thump, thump* of God's surprising activity in our lives—grace that is so surprising because it is so far beyond what we could ever imagine or ask for.

I wonder what would have happened if those early Christians hadn't opened the door. What if the fear of bad news had so overwhelmed them that they never answered Peter's knock because they were scared or even cynical? They would have missed the miracle standing out there waiting to be let in. But please understand. Our expectation *does not determine* what God will or will not do. Our expectation of the *thump, thump, thump* of God's miracles in our lives keeps us from recognizing what God is already doing in our lives and paves the way for our participation in God's miracles with joy.

You know that there are many *thump, thump, thumps* of God's activity all around us today—amazing answers to people's prayers. We don't engage in empty pious formality when we pray. On the contrary, when we pray, we are in touch with someone so wonderful. The living God is at work in our midst bringing the *thump, thump, thump* of his surprising activity to our door over and over again. And I want to encourage you to begin expecting so that you don't miss the joy and excitement of participating fully in what God is doing.

Here are a few suggestions that may nurture that very expectation in your prayer life, even when the chips are down:

(1) Begin thanking God for acting on your behalf before you see an immediate answer to prayer. This is a faith stance that God is able to handle whatever we pray for, no matter how overwhelming or painful the circumstances may be.

(2) Soak up scriptures that describe the Lord's nature, scriptures such as:

- Steadfast love surrounds those who trust in the Lord. (Psalm 32:10 NRSV)
- There is now no condemnation for those who are in Christ Jesus. (Romans 8:1)
- In all these things we are more than conquerors through him who loved us. (Romans 8:37)

It starts you thinking, "If I belong to such a loving God, then I can't help expecting God to act on my behalf and surprise me with grace!"

(3) Finally, in the context of prayer, dare to take risks for Jesus Christ as he calls you to do so. Give a little more than you think you can. Take a stand when no one else will. Your expectation of his faithfulness to you will open your eyes to his sufficiency in every situation and will increase your expectancy many times over.

When I was working as a chaplain in a local psychiatric facility, my supervisor told me not to pray with my patients, because it would give them false hope. We didn't want them to expect too much from God, he said, and then get disappointed. I followed his advice for a while until Frank, one of the patients, got the better of me. Every time I walked into that locked men's ward that smelled of cigarettes and sweat, Frank would meet me, sobbing. "Have you come to take me home, Kim?" he would cry. "Have you come to take me home?" His drool would mix with his tears and his hands would shake as he grabbed my arm. After about six months of that, I could take it no longer. Glancing around furtively one day, making sure that my supervisor was nowhere in sight, I said a very quick, curt prayer for Frank. I even dared to pray that God would make it possible for him to go home—whatever that meant for him. Several days later when I returned, Frank was not there. *Thump, thump, thump.* "The most amazing thing happened," the nurse told me when I asked about his whereabouts. "We didn't realize Frank had any family, but his sister has evidently been looking for his whereabouts for years. She arrived the other day, visited, worked out all the details, and took him home."

What an amazing God we worship! There is no false hope with

God. Rather, the *thump, thump, thump* of God's surprises at our doorstep pounds out the truth that we worship a living reality who is actively and powerfully at work in the world. God is able to do exceedingly and abundantly over all that we ask or think, no matter what the circumstance. So we ought to be ready for anything!

Questions for Reflection

1. What was the greatest surprise that God ever gave you?

2. How can we increase our expectancy that God does hear and does act when we pray? What scriptures do you find helpful for reminding you of this?

3. How does thanking God before we receive what we ask for make sense and go beyond just a Pollyannish denial of the problem?

4. Where might you use greater expectancy in your prayer life?

Dear Jesus, I do not always pray expectantly. Often, when you answer my prayers, I am shocked. Give me the gift of faith, so that when I pray I will know that you hear me and will begin to act on my behalf immediately. Thank you for being a God of surprises and of the unexpected. What an amazing adventure it is to walk and follow you. In Jesus' name, I pray. Amen.

Chapter 4

Seeing Jesus When He Seems Far Away

"When the Mist Rises"

Isaiah 7:14; Luke 2:25-32

When I was young, my family and I lived in Switzerland for a year. If you continued farther up the hill on the road where we lived, there was a large field on one side. The villagers who lived in that area told us that on a clear day you could see a magnificent view of Mont Blanc across that field. Mont Blanc, or Mount White, was known in Switzerland as the highest of the Alps. But try as we might, we couldn't catch a glimpse of it. Every time we would drive up to the field, the mist hung low, the clouds were heavy, and all we could see was an empty field. After a while, we stopped journeying up that way, wondering if perhaps the view was a bit over-rated anyway, a kind of exaggeration meant to trap naive Americans into renting houses close by. But one early morning, we journeyed up that hill again, and the mists were gone. There the mountain stood—a great jagged peak soaring up to the sky, flashing reds and pinks from the rising sun. It was a magnificent view! Although our subsequent trips to the field were obstructed by heavy mist more often than not, we had seen that alpine giant once and the vision of it stayed with us. Occasionally, on a clear day it would greet us with grandeur once again. But even when we couldn't see the mountain, we knew it was there.[1]

Since I am not a very good cook and am not a shopper, the intrinsic joy that some people experience doing these things eludes me completely. I find it difficult to sense God's presence in these ways, especially in certain stores, waiting in line, on certain days—such as in the bargain stores that I tend to frequent that have no atmosphere and no prices on anything. And though I try to cook, when my ten-year-old gently suggests that maybe Daddy could make dinner, I'm not the least bit inclined to try my hand at the recipes in the family magazines. So my joy in the maintenance mode of life can easily turn to feelings of obligation and duty. That's where I lose my vision of Jesus. That's where I miss the mark and become blinded by the mist of routine, rather than inspired by the vision of the God who is there—if only I could stop long enough to see it and to reclaim that joy.

In the swirling mist of all of the activity we are involved in, we often lose sight of the face of Jesus Christ. Yet he is always with us, available and ready to be in relationship with us. It is my hope that we would not have our spiritual plane of vision obstructed by the busyness and cacophony of day-to-day routine and miss the profound magnificence of what life is all about: God bends down to us in Jesus Christ as an infant in a manger, in a way that wouldn't frighten us. God whispers in our ear, "I love you, I love you, I love you." And the thing that breaks my heart year after year as I walk with the Lord is the searing awareness that God's longing for me is far more passionate and pure than my longing for God will ever be. I become so frustrated with myself when I let the mist of activity and busyness define me in such shallow ways, though the call of God's love is all that I really want. But I do it all the time. I miss the vision of his face longing for relationship and communion with me. I get distracted and miss the "God with us—Emmanuel" message. In the story of Jesus' visit to Mary and Martha's house in Luke, Martha became anxious and stirred up a bunch of mist as she worried about many things when only one thing was needful— to see and be in relationship with Jesus.

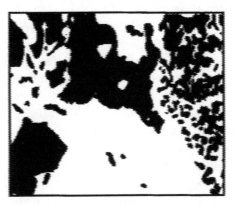

The picture above may at first look like nothing to you. You may simply see a lot of blobs floating around, perhaps unconsciously representative of islands of activity and stress in our lives. But if you look carefully for a while, you will see the face of Christ in the center top portion. You have to know where to focus and you have to spend a little time doing it. Certain things have to recede and other things come to the foreground so that the image can become clear. This is not a test of whether you are going to heaven or not. This has nothing to do with IQ or a standard by which your spiritual maturity will be measured. This example simply illustrates how close our Lord is, and yet how we can miss seeing him altogether in the midst of the clutter and terminal busyness of our days. Jesus is here now. Experiencing (or seeing) him in the moment, allowing the mist to rise and the fog in our brain to clear and the vision to emerge clearly and distinctly, allowing certain things to recede and allowing other things to take priority, means a certain amount of effort in terms of focus and perspective. But it's worth it once you see the *face of Christ;* and when you do, it is such a joy. It's an "Aha!" experience and that is what every day will become for us when we see Jesus in the center of it all.

If you've seen the mountain behind the mist even once you know it's there, no matter how many foggy, difficult days there are afterward. Many people have said to me, "I want to see God—I want to believe, but I just don't feel God's presence." Stress and uncertainty about the future can cause the clouds to hang heavy and block out the greater vision of God's presence. Life is difficult. There are many times in our lives when we don't feel God's presence. But I always ask people going through the hard times if they've ever, as far back as they can remember, had an experience in which the mist rose for them and they knew that God was there. Usually a story tumbles out about a better time when the vision of God's love was more distinct. One woman teared up and said, "My grandmother used to sing to me, 'Jesus loves me, this I know' when

I was three years old. That's the last time I remember knowing that I was loved by someone beyond myself. But it was so real. That's why I'm back here at church, thirty years later, trying to figure out what it all means." When has the mist risen for you? When have you been aware of God's presence with you? of God's love for you? calling you? Because that's the reality we celebrate as Christians.

When has the mist risen in your life? If you've experienced the Lord's presence in your life, even if it was years ago, on some level, you know he's there—calling to you even now. Like the mountain, God doesn't move—we do! If you've never had an experience of the mist rising, of Jesus touching your life in an intimate, personal way, all you have to do is open your heart to Jesus Christ to experience the love and grace you were created to receive.

Blaise Pascal, a brilliant French philosopher-mathematician who lived in the seventeenth century, learned how to touch, hear, and see his creator. He had formerly sought God with his intellect alone but had a conversion experience that changed his life. So powerful was this experience that Pascal wrote it down and sewed it inside his coat so that he could physically touch that experience and remember its reality. This experience sustained Pascal through a myriad of struggles. Each time he would falter or feel that he was losing touch with that vision of God, he would touch the portion of his coat where he had sewn the account of his experience with God, and he would rejoice. Nine years after this experience, Pascal died, and what he had written was found on his clothing. It went like this:

Monday, 23 of November from 10:30 until about 12:30 at night. . . .
It felt like fire. God of Abraham, God of Isaac, God of Jacob. Not the

God of philosophers and scholars. Certainty, joy, peace, God of Jesus Christ. He is only found along the ways that are taught in the gospel. Tears of joy. I had parted from Him. Let me never be separated from Him. Surrender to Jesus Christ.[2]

Perhaps Pascal's actions seem a bit odd, and yet the physical touching of that experience reminded him that there was a different way of seeing things, another voice to listen to rather than his own logic and philosophy. There was a bigger vision, a larger plan, a wonderful God who had called him, and a passion ran deep inside him never to be separated from or lose sight of that vision and experience of God.

When has the mist risen for you? Hold on to that vision of Jesus. Nurture it. Believe in it. Give your life to it. We don't see it all clearly in this life. These are the "shadowlands" as C. S. Lewis put it. Paul says, "Now we see but a poor reflection as in a mirror; then we shall see face to face. Now I know in part; then I shall know fully, even as I am fully known" (1 Corinthians 13:12). Until we see Jesus face-to-face, we must hold on to those holy moments when the mist has risen and our vision is clear. And these glimpses of the Lord are enough. "If you could see what I see," a saintly woman told me just before she died, "and hear what I hear, you would not weep for me."

Questions for Reflection

1. Recall a time when you most felt or knew that God was with you. How would you describe this experience?

2. Recall a time when God felt far away. Did the experience recalled above or a similar experience help you through this period of time?

3. If you are feeling far from God, what is most helpful in recovering a sense of his presence?

4. What is the primary thing you long to know that now seems to be dim and unclear?

These prayer suggestions have been adapted from Brennan Manning's book, *The Signature of Jesus*.[3] Find a quiet ten minutes to pray in this way each day. As you do, you will be amazed how the less important, distracting elements recede and how the face of Christ becomes preeminent just as in the inkblot. Ten minutes may seem like a long time at first, but eventually ten minutes will hardly seem long enough.

(1) Take a few minutes to relax your body and quiet your spirit.

(2) Choose a single word or phrase that captures the flavor of your relationship with God. Examples might be:

> Good Shepherd
> God with us/me
> Master
> Comforter
> Divine Friend

(3) Repeat the word inwardly, slowly, and often. When distractions come, as they inevitably will, simply return your focus to the single word or phrase you have chosen.

After a ten-minute period of prayer, conclude with the Lord's Prayer, a favorite verse or psalm, or some spontaneous words of praise and thanks. Even the words of Simeon, "My eyes have seen your salvation" (Luke 2:30).

You can't go wrong when you take the time to focus on Jesus. Once you see the face of Christ in the inkblot, you know that it is there, even if you didn't see it before. Once you experience the passionate love of God for you in Jesus Christ, the mist has risen and the wonderful joy of being in relationship with your Creator begins.

Dear Jesus, help me hold on to the vision of you that I have experienced, even when the wilderness threatens to dry up my faith. I know that the mist will rise again for me, and I look forward to the day I will see you face to face. In Jesus' name. Amen.

Chapter 5

Seeing Jesus in the Storms

"In the Stern of the Boat"

Luke 8:22-25

At first glance there doesn't seem to be anything remarkable about Luke's account of the disciples' journey to the other side of the Sea of Galilee. The day was probably relatively calm, so no one thought it a life-threatening task to climb into the boat and journey peacefully across the Sea of Galilee. They had probably done it many times before. As they set sail, Jesus settled himself in the stern of the boat and fell asleep. Finally, away from the crowds and the clamor, Almighty God stretched out to rest.

They sailed quietly for a while, but suddenly, without a warning, a storm hit the tiny fishing vessel. The waves slapped the wooden sideboards, and the wind, rising up out of nowhere, began to churn the waters and whip the sails. The sky grew dark, and rain began to pelt down on the disciples. The raging, foaming waves stirred up from the deep grew larger and darker, until their impact jolted the boat from side to side, spilling water onto the deck and ripping the sails. In other words, it was no *small* storm that Luke talks about here. It is no brief thundershower. Many of the disciples were seasoned fishermen who were familiar with the ways of the wind and water. They knew how to handle themselves in a boat. They'd been in many a storm and steered their vessels safely to shore. So this storm must have been bad enough to cause experienced fishermen to panic. It must have threatened to tear their boat in pieces or smash them into the rocks. They frantically begin to bail out water and struggled to secure the tattered sail. Over the sound of the wind, they shout to one another—where was their Master? Was he panicking? Was he among them, drenched, holding a bucket, and shouting orders? No. Almighty God was asleep in the stern of the boat. In the midst of all the activity, the panic, the violent thrashing of wind and water, Jesus sleeps undisturbed.

Now, I get upset when the kitchen is messy and I am trying to clean dried food off the dishes while my husband, Tim, is snoring away on the couch in blissful contentment. How much worse for the disciples, who found themselves in a life-and-death situation! They must have been beside themselves with fear. During it all, Jesus continues to sleep, completely oblivious to the storm swirling around him. How could he sleep through such violence? Didn't he hear their cries and feel the trembling of the feeble boat that was being tossed like cork along the surface of the water? I think it's interesting that the disciples waited *so long* before rousing him. They did everything they could think of *first* before finally waking Jesus. By that point, they were finally convinced that they were going to perish: "Master, Master, we're going to drown!" (Luke

8:24). Mark's Gospel reads, "Teacher, don't you care if we drown?" (Mark 4:38).

Does the disciples' anguished plea sound familiar? Have you ever thought and said those same things to God in the midst of trouble or in a crisis or at the brink of a failure? "God, don't you care? Are you asleep? Wake up, God!" I have. How does Jesus respond to the disciples? Does he yell, "Abandon ship"? Does he panic and join the disciples in their frenzied attempt to salvage the sinking vessel? Does he roll over, grunt, and say, "Sorry, guys, but I'm in the middle of a lovely dream so don't bother me." No. He got up, rebuked the wind and the water, and the storm subsided. Everything became quiet. He looked from one ragged disciple to the next, as they stood dumbfounded by this demonstration of power. Only God could command the waves and wind. So who was Jesus, this man who had such power? "Where is your faith?" he asked them. "Where is your faith?"

My Bible has headings above all of the scripture passages, which help me find things I'm looking for as I leaf through Scripture. For this particular passage, I have an italicized heading that reads, "Jesus Calms the Storm." That's very true, and it's usually the point we focus on when we read this story. But I think the point of this story is not simply that Jesus could still the storm, but rather that the disciples should have trusted his power to help them from the outset. Like the disciples, we also temporarily forget from time to time that God is always there, resting in the stern of our boat. Almighty God, the creator of all things, is far more available and competent than I am apt to realize. Why is it that so often I wait until I am drowning to cry for help?

Our fear makes it so easy to lose our focus. It is easy to get distracted and pay more attention to the storm than to Jesus, as the disciples did. And by storm I mean any number of things that might assail us, bringing panic, fear, chaos, and distress. A storm in our midst could be something as commonplace as a jam-packed day at the office (or church), or it could be something more severe like the loss of a loved one or a serious medical difficulty or the loss of a job or the breakup of a marriage.

And there are at least three things that make these storms particularly frightening and distressing.

First, storms generate a lot of sounds that are out of the ordinary. The question my children ask the most during a storm is, "What's that noise?" repeated approximately every two minutes all night long! There's howling, groaning, creaking, and thunder. A lot of extra noise also occurs during our own difficult times because of friction or conflict in our relationships or life circumstances. These noises can be not only frightening, but also exhausting to process and deal with.

Second, storms show us that what we thought was secure isn't. During a recent storm in my area, things that were supposed to be stationary flew around, such as chairs and tree limbs and awnings. After the storm was over, the street outside our house was a mess. In the same way, the things that make us feel secure—things such as jobs, finances, or relationships that you thought would always be there—can suddenly disappear.

Finally, storms immobilize us. They prevent us from getting where we want to go, even if it's just to the other side of the lake. It's easy to ask in the midst of a storm, "Where's my life going anyway?" It's tempting to give in to despair and resign oneself to lost dreams and a hopeless future. Perhaps the most frightening thing about storms is that they demonstrate the absolute fragility of what we depend on to keep ourselves feeling powerful and in control.

During these times, we have difficulty remembering and focusing on the peaceful companion resting in our boat. As the familiar saying goes, "Why pray when you can worry?" We often choose worry perhaps because it gives us the illusion that we are doing something and that we can control things. But when we do, we also choose stormy weather, thereby increasing our fear and anxiety. What if next time you faced a storm, instead of choosing worry you choose to remember that Almighty God is present in the stern of your boat and is our only true source of power and security. Perhaps we might think differently and say, "Why worry when you can pray?"

Probably the closest I have ever come to the panic-stricken state of the disciples in that boat occurred on a camping trip in a remote area, high in the Adirondack Mountains. One night, Tim and I were sleeping in our pop-up, two-person, special-value tent and were awakened by a noise in the campsite. Shining a light outside, we saw a bear cub frolicking around the fire pit. No big deal. We were avid campers and had been around bears before. No problem until junior bear cub managed to knock down our backpacks that had been hoisted up a tree. When the backpacks fell, Junior got scared and ran off, probably to find his mom. Moments later, an angry she-bear roared into the campsite and began throwing whatever she could get her hands on—logs, rocks, backpacks. We began a frenzied effort to scare her off by banging pots, yelling, and shining lights in her direction. Rather than running away, as she was supposed to, she charged our tent and began circling it, growling and banging into the sides. I never realized that bears had such bad breath until the moment she pressed against the vinyl side of the tent, crushing it inward so that it was only inches from my face, and roared. We had banged all the pots and made all the noise we could. There was nothing left to do but pray: "Lord, don't you care that we're dying? Help us! Please!" All we had to do was ask. After that simple crisis prayer, we were enveloped in a palpable peace. The words from Psalm 91:10 immediately came to mind: "No harm will befall you, no disaster will come near your tent" (even if it was a pop-up, two-person, special-value tent). At that moment, inexplicably the wind began to blow, perhaps dispersing our scent, and the bear—who still had her head pressed hard against the tent—slowly began to retreat. Finally, after what seemed like an eternity, she crashed off into the woods.

You'd think that after an experience like that, I'd never again doubt the power of Jesus Christ to calm more normal, everyday kinds of storms. But often I still find myself anxiously bailing out the boat before going to Jesus in prayer. It's so easy to forget that God is present and available amidst the storms and in the hassles of everyday life and has the resources to help us, even in crisis situations. Recently a friend called me and told me that in prayer she had felt this warm presence surrounding her, and after it left, a stomach ailment that had been causing her excruciating pain had disappeared. "It's strange," she said, "but while it was happening, it seemed so real. Now it's as if I can hardly believe it actually happened—except I have no more pain. I need constantly to remind myself that God is there for me to call on in any and all situations." We sometimes find it difficult to grasp God's nearness and availability. At such times, we need to think consciously about focusing on God, centering ourselves in God's presence, and remembering God's goodness and mercy. We can be assured that when we cry out to God, we will never get an answering machine message saying that God is unavailable or away from the office. God is always available, closer than we think, and so powerful to help.

You've probably heard the old proverb that says God helps those who help themselves, but you *won't* find it in Scripture. The truth is that God helps those who can't help themselves and know that they can't. Only after the disciples had exhausted their own efforts did they cry out to the only one who *really* could help them. Sometimes storms make you realize just how dependent you are on the power of Jesus.

The author of Hebrews tells us to "fix your thoughts on Jesus, the apostle and high priest whom we confess" (3:1). But how do we fix our thoughts on Jesus? I've been a Christian for a long time. But no matter how many years I have known with my head that Jesus is in the stern of the boat ready to help me, it's a different thing actually to trust him with whatever stormy circumstances I may be up against. It takes a real resolve to focus on Jesus rather than on the scary, noisy storm that's swirling around me and keeping me from getting anywhere.

The six Rs for focusing on Jesus in the recklessness of the storm has helped me bridge the gap between what I know in my head and actually trusting the Lord with my life in difficult times.

This is *how* we fix our eyes on Jesus:

1. ***Read*** scriptures that talk about God's deliverance. As David does in Psalm 86, you, too, can call to God in your day of trouble and be assured of an answer.

2. *Receive* from the Lord in prayer.
3. *Remember* what God has done for you in the past to bring you where you are today.
4. *Recognize* that God never changes. Jesus is available to help you through your storm just as he was on that stormy day on the lake with his disciples.
5. *Rejoice* that the Lord uses even the storms of our lives to draw us closer to him.
6. *Reach* out to others who can support and encourage you in the faith.

The same hands that created the winds and the waves and brought peace to the troubled waters were driven through with iron stakes for you and me, so that we could call to him when storms threaten to capsize our fragile worlds. Almighty God abides with you in the stern of your boat today just as he did for the disciples and stands ready to act on your behalf. God calls us to stop bailing out all that water and fighting the storm by ourselves against forces that only God can calm. Give God your life. Relinquish your storms. God is present, right here in the stern of our boat.

Questions for Reflection

1. What has been the most recent storm you have experienced? Did you experience noise? Did you realize that things you thought were secure weren't or that you couldn't get where you needed to go?

2. Was it more natural to focus on the storm or on God? Why do you think this is?

3. Which of the six Rs for focusing on Jesus in the midst of the storm has been most helpful for you? Which has been the least helpful?

4. Given the fact that life is filled with storms, how might you prepare yourself ahead of time for the next one?

Dear Jesus, your love and presence are all that I need to get through the storms of my life. Forgive me for being so afraid of the waves that I forget how close you are. Give me the courage and faith to focus on you and to trust you with my life. In your name, I pray. Amen.

Chapter 6

Seeing Jesus
in the Mustard Seeds

Matthew 17:20; Luke 13:18-19; 1 Corinthians 1:27-29

Scripture compares the kingdom of God to things we might not expect: small things such as pearls, little children, lost coins, and being faithful in the small things we do. God's kingdom is all about insignificant beginnings that have earth-shattering results. It reminds me of the scripture that says, "But God chose the foolish things of the world to shame the wise; God chose the weak things of the world to shame the strong. He chose the lowly things of this world and the despised things—and the things that are not—to nullify the things that are, so that no one may boast before him" (1 Corinthians 1:27-29).

If you tried to define the kingdom of heaven, you might say that it is the place where God's perfect intent claims the order of things. Of course, in God's kingdom the "normal" order of this world is radically reversed. What images does the word *kingdom* conjure up for you? What do you associate with power and might? I imagine turrets and towers, flags, thick walls, and majestic leaders in flowing robes leading great battles to preserve the large area of conquest that they call their own. Mustard seeds, old coins lost in dusty corners, and children clamoring for attention hardly fit into that framework. And yet Jesus tells us that the kingdom of heaven is precisely like *this*. It is a place where the weak are made strong, where the lost and outcast are found and given a home, where the powerful and mighty are made weak.

God isn't threatened by the evil and rancor in our world. Jesus creates his kingdom from things we would consider fit only for the reject bin, the secondhand store, or the discard heap to bring about his intent and to show us his glory. He works through a manger, from a dinner in a thief's home, through a weeping prostitute, and from a cursed cross, transforming them and creating God's kingdom from them. What we wouldn't expect he uses; what we had thought insignificant, weak, and undignified becomes significant, strong, and valuable through the transforming power of God's love.

I am in ministry today only because a small child from the slums of Harlem melted my icy frozen will. I was absolutely dead set against going to seminary. Until the encounter with this child, I had successfully managed to ignore the urging of the Holy Spirit.

There are so many clergy in my family that we had nine ministers in our wedding so that we wouldn't hurt anybody's feelings. Even deciding who would say grace each Thanksgiving was a monumental task. By the time I was a teenager, I was so churched out I would rather have been dissecting mosquito larvae in a tropical jungle than going to the nicest church in town. I was bound and determined to do my own thing. We already had more than enough clergy in the family.

On a particularly humid day, Tim and I moved out of New York City. We had graduated from college and were off to new vistas. Our rented apartment was in the middle of an area of Harlem that poor students could afford. I couldn't wait to leave. I wanted to leave behind the cockroach-infested kitchen, the profanity screamed across the airshaft, the garbage dumped out of windows, the person who stole our stereo, and the rooster who lived upstairs and crowed himself silly at two in the afternoon. Of course, leaving also meant we had to say good-bye to the children in the neighborhood—the children who we had told about Jesus, the children who had come over for snacks, the children who loved to roller-skate up and down our long warped wooden hallway. On that humid moving day, nine-year-old Maximo was watching me pack with the searing eyes of a prophet. Maximo, who was small for his age and not too bright by the school's standards, had been labeled a "problem child." I remember him as if it were yesterday. He had one roller skate on, the other off, hair pointing out in all directions. "You'll forget us, you know," he whispered. "You're going on to a better life, but we have to stay here. One day when you're enjoying yourself, you might look up and say to your husband, 'Remember all those kids?' You might do that once. But you'll forget us, you know." In that mustard-seed moment the Holy Spirit hit me like a shot. From the bowels of Harlem, from a small child who had been rejected one too many times, came this earthshaking awareness that melted the ice around my frozen heart so stiffly and rigidly committed to doing my own thing. In that moment, looking into his face, I knew I couldn't just go my own way. In Max's face, I saw the face of Jesus Christ and knew I belonged to him. It was not my choice to go to seminary, but I went.

A similar occurrence happened when we were on a mission trip to Mexico. At the time, my son Jonathan was only six, so I almost decided not to take him on the trip. I had an image of him pounding in a nail and a half and then wanting lunch. But he worked hard. We nailed and painted and got to know the people. When it was over and we were coming home from the airport, Jonathan mentioned casually as I was attending to something else, "You know, Mom, when we were praying in the church, a Mexican woman was holding my hand and I felt something." That got my attention. "What do you mean when you say you felt something?" I asked, trying to sound nonchalant and not wanting to bias his response. "Well," he said matter-of-factly, "it was like God came into me from her. I was all tingly. God is never going to forget about me, you know."

First, for Jonathan to say that he would never be forgotten was huge because as the third and youngest child in our family, he can often feel as if he is forgotten.

Second, had I been able to articulate my heart's desire, it would have been that my child would experience in a personal way the reality of the Holy Spirit in his life. And here it came from a woman I don't even know, who lived in the depths of material poverty in Mexico. Her city was dotted with shacks, barbed wire, and trash, yet she gave my son the greatest treasure I could ever ask for. By worldly standards this woman was poor, but by spiritual standards, rich. Earthshaking tremors in the kingdom of heaven begin with tiny mustard seeds, small children, lost coins, or pearls. God uses the weak things of the world to confound the strong.

We have to be alert and vigilant or we might miss God at work in the world. God's power and might to change the world comes in the humblest of ways—through the smallest things, through people we might turn away from, in the midst of interruptions, and in the still, small voice of the Holy Spirit whispering in our ear. I believe God often works in such small, mysterious ways to keep us from believing that we are responsible solely by virtue of our own efforts. Accomplishing wonderful and powerful things through such unlikely people and events also demonstrates just how victorious God really is.

Recently, a woman in my office opened her heart to receive Jesus. It was the last thing I expected because I was in a rush, had a million things to do, and felt decidedly unspiritual. As I was rushing around, I handed her a Bible and began to tell her quickly about Jesus. She looked up at me, her eyes glistening, patted my hand, and said, "It's okay. I actually can feel him and it is enough." God uses even my weakest moments for glory. The times when I know I can give only a mustard seed are so often the times during which God chooses to act. This knowledge humbles me, reminding me that "my ministry" is really about what God is doing *through* me.

It's hard to have singularity of purpose when there are so many more choices now than ever before and promises for happiness based on acquisition and distraction. Recently someone shared an important insight they had discovered (through Christian counseling): "You know, I realize that all the stuff I have been investing myself in really is not that important in the long run. I work with money a lot, for instance, but what I really want to know is how to grow deeper in my faith so that I can feel connected to God."

That posture of seeking first God's priorities, of discovering what is meaningful to God, is the first step in cracking the ice and moving mountains. Once you realize that God's kingdom is worth pursuing, you can let go and allow God to work through you.

There are some practical ways to begin living the kind of faithful service that will allow God to move mountains using mustard seeds.

1. Do one small thing with great love each day and keep it up.

If we all did that, just within our church, the warmth of the Holy Spirit would melt so much ice around us we'd be amazed. I know that it is far easier to say than to do. It's easy to discredit mustard seeds, to look down on them, to shake your head and declare, "My small act of service just isn't enough even if God is in charge." You wonder how such a small act of service can make any difference in light of all of the poverty and desperation in the world.

The disciples faced a crowd of 5,000 hungry people with only two smelly fish and five barley loaves. In their desperation they cried out, "Lord, what are these small food items among so many?" But Jesus took the smelly fish and the five barley loaves in his hands, blessed them, multiplied them, and everyone was fed. It wasn't important how many resources they had. Rather it was in whose hands those mustard seed resources were held. Pursue God's kingdom, allow God to use your mustard seed resources, and watch mountains move.

2. Pursue the mustard seed on your doorstep.

Who or what has God put on your doorstep? Is it an elderly parent you must persevere in caring for? Is it a child into whom you are pouring your energies and whom you are worried about? Maybe you're desperately working to save your marriage, or you're hanging on to the hope that one day God will answer a prayer that has been on your heart for years. Continuing may not be an easy thing to do, but it may be exactly the task to which God calls you.

3. Persevere in prayer.

God calls us all to pursue the mustard seed of prayer. There is nothing more powerful. I want to encourage you to commit to praying for ten minutes every day, praying for one thing in our world that concerns you. Resist the temptation to believe that your prayers don't *really* matter. Watch for the miracles of mustard seeds and pursue them, for through these small acts will the world be transformed into the kingdom of God.

Questions for Reflection

1. Why do you think God uses the small, weak, and often unattractive things to bring about change in the world? How did God use the manger? the cross?

2. What things must you do on a regular basis that can feel insignificant and futile? How might these duties or responsibilities be transformed?

3. Mother Teresa said that we ought to seek to do not great things, but "small things with great love." What does that mean for you?

4. How can we stay awake so that we don't miss the significance of God at work in the simple, ordinary, small things of our lives?

Lord, give me eyes to see what you are doing in and through the very smallest, weakest venues that I might otherwise reject. Show me, in my own life what it means to do small things with great love, so that I can be a mustard seed provider for your glory and honor. In Jesus' name. Amen.

Chapter 7

Seeing Jesus When You Are
"Out on a Limb"

Luke 19:1-9

When was the last time you climbed a tree? I think I was about nine years old the last time I climbed one. The tree I climbed was at a local park and was about sixty feet high. When you reached the top, you would sway back and forth in the wind. The last time I climbed that tree, I was trying to discover whether the earth was round from that great height. I thought perhaps I might get a glimpse of our planet, tilting and twirling through space. But the world still looked flat, even from up there. But after climbing the sycamore tree, Zacchaeus was never to see the world or himself the same way again. Not after Jesus came along.

Zacchaeus wanted to see Jesus so badly that he ran ahead of the crowd and climbed a tree. Can't you just see that little man, tearing down the dusty street, his rich robes flying out behind him, his sandals pounding furiously across the ground? Can you imagine him hoisting himself clumsily into that tree, beads of sweat on his forehead, and clinging precariously to a limb? All that trouble was worth it just to be able to see Jesus as he passed by with the crowd.

Zacchaeus was physically short so he needed the height of the tree to see over the crowd. But I think that deep inside he was also aware that he "fell short," so to speak. Given who he was, a tax collector who cheated others, he may have felt destined to observe Jesus from a distance. He was not just any tax collector either; he was the chief tax collector and a very wealthy man, which meant he also had a bunch of other cheats working for him. And in all of this he knew he had done wrong. So just a distant, passing glance of Jesus was probably all that he was hoping for. But even that glimmer of hope, as small as it was, made him charge ahead of the crowd and climb a tree.

It is then that Jesus miraculously calls Zacchaeus by name; he already knows Zacchaeus. Zacchaeus thought he was looking for Jesus, but Jesus had been looking for him all along. Jesus saw through Zacchaeus's wealth and riches. He knew that Zacchaeus was more than the things he had done wrong. He perceived that Zacchaeus climbed the tree because he longed to be more than he had become. Then Jesus invites himself over! He wants to go home with Zacchaeus and share a meal with him. Can't you hear Jesus saying to Zacchaeus, "Forget the tree, the aerial view. Let's relax together and share in fellowship. I know you, Zacchaeus. Open your home and get to know me."

Sharing a meal with Zacchaeus was a pretty radical act on Jesus' part. If you had been among those in the crowd, could you understand why this might rub you the wrong way? You would probably wonder why Jesus chose to spend time with a short little man who robbed your neighbors, taking their last coins and leaving them hungry. "The Pharisees turned up their noses. Who is this man that eats with tax collectors and sinners? How dare he!" (Mark 2:16, my paraphrase).

Do you see how Jesus cuts through all the distorted behavior and motivation that had defined Zacchaeus up to that point, pays not one iota of attention to the criticism of the self-consciously righteous, and believes instead that the deepest longing of Zacchaeus's heart was to have fellowship with him?

If you identify with Zacchaeus, if you want a closer walk with God today, what keeps you out on a limb? What causes you to settle for an aerial view, a brief passing glimpse of God, simultaneously longing for God's presence but unable to unlock the door of your heart? God wants to enter our homes and our hearts and desires nothing more than to have communion with us.

Maybe you are out on a limb because . . .

Circumstances seem to indicate that God does not care. Hurtful circumstances can make the padlock to our heart very stiff and painful to unlock.

Let me tell you about a time when I was out on a limb and felt that God didn't care. Although we do have three children now, Tim and I had been trying to get pregnant for many years before we became pregnant with our first child. We were so excited. Our families were excited. We began to plan and anticipate, and everyone said what a wonderful answer to prayer this was. Then I got the chicken pox for the first time in my life and the baby inside me died. What had I done to deserve that? Was it sin in my life? Was it that God didn't care? One very religious person even suggested that perhaps it happened because God knew I wouldn't be a good mother. This event didn't stop me from believing in God, but suddenly I found myself way up the tree, trying to see God's presence in the midst of those circumstances, but from a great distance. I questioned my call to ministry. I became skeptical and critical. When people would ask me if I wanted to pray, I would say, "No, you pray."

Jesus never stopped calling me down from my distant perch out on a limb. He kept saying, "Hey, can I come over? Will you just open the door a crack and let me into your pain so I can help?" But I was very stubborn and refused; I was so hurt. I don't know what your need is, but no matter where you are, remember that Jesus is available and will come if you pray: "God make yourself real for me. I don't understand it all, but come as you promised and give me rest."

The Lord intervenes in each situation and in different ways for each person, but here is what God did for me. One day, while I was still hurt and confused, copies of my old medical charts ended up in my hands. The medical charts told me a story. When I was two years old, I evidently put the loose end of an electric cord in my mouth (the other end was plugged into the wall socket), and the inside of my mouth was burned, turning completely white. I was rushed to Boston Children's Hospital where a specialist in electric burns told my parents that I would probably never speak again, and if I did I would suffer from a speech impediment and deformity on the outside of my mouth as well. As I flipped through the chart, the doctor's scrawl went on two years later. He couldn't explain why I managed to come out of this experience unscathed and wrote something about the power of prayer and guardian angels.

The timing couldn't have been better. The Lord knew I needed to see that medical chart right then because reading that account made me clamber down out of the tree and back into his arms. "Okay, Lord," I said, "you can come over. My heart is your home again." Reading that account made me aware that despite painful circumstances in my life that I still don't understand, God had a plan and a purpose for me and I belonged to him no matter what.

He has a plan and a purpose for your life, too. Regardless of the circumstances, Jesus is inviting himself over right now. "Hey, can I come over?" he asks you. "If you'd just come on down from that branch up there, open the door that's holding back whatever it is that's keeping us apart, maybe then we can have fellowship together and an honest conversation."

You've had a hard time forgiving yourself for something.

Zacchaeus was surprised, given his history, that Jesus would even stop to give him the time of day. Though Zacchaeus was the chief of cheating tax collectors, we have no record of Jesus pointing his finger or making him feel guilty. There are no spiritual laws recited. There is no mandate—just Jesus' request for fellowship. In response, Zacchaeus vows to give up half of everything he has and to repay those whom he has cheated four times the amount he owes. This was an extravagant gesture, the absolute extreme of what the law required, in response to Jesus' extravagant love for him. Salvation had come to his house!

Anne Lamott, a popular speaker and author, was also surprised that Jesus gave her the time of day given her past. Before she met

Jesus, she was addicted to cocaine and alcohol and was involved in an affair that produced a child that she aborted. She found herself spiraling downward, disgusted with herself. How on earth could anybody love her now? Lying in bed one night, she suddenly felt Jesus in the room. She describes it this way:

> I felt him [one night] just sitting there . . . watching me with patience and love, and I squinched my eyes shut, but that didn't help because that's not what I was seeing him with. . . . [After that] everywhere I went, I had the feeling that a little cat was following me . . . wanting me to open the door and let it in. But I knew what would happen: you let a cat in one time, give it a little milk, and it stays forever. . . . [Finally] I hung my head and said . . . "I quit." I took a long deep breath and said out loud, "All right. You can come in." So this was my beautiful moment of conversion.[1]

Talk about inviting himself over! Jesus wouldn't leave her alone. We all may look pretty good on the outside, but most of us carry things that others can't see. No matter what has happened in your past, what you've done, who you've been with, or what you're going through now, Jesus wants to invite himself over: "Come down from the tree. The present is now and if I could just come over, you could get to know me for the first time or all over again. Let me into the home of your heart." God has forgiven you of your past. You can forgive yourself.

Maybe you're out on a limb today because you're skeptical.
Usually skepticism also stems from hurt of some sort: an authoritarian Bible thumper who made us shiver as a child, a church with a myopic worldview, a navel-gazing Bible study, or a Pollyannish faith. Those distorted views of God and religion are out there, but

don't let them define the reality of who Jesus is. Human beings do the best they can, but we are all broken and fall short.

Your skepticism may stem from the fact that you are approaching your relationship with Jesus from an intellectual point of view. An intellectual grasp of faith is very different from grasping its meaning in your heart. It's like the difference between hearing about Hawaii and actually going there—which would you rather do? A woman recently told me that she had really grasped God's love for the first time—not just as something she knew about, but as something she experienced. She had just gone through a long battle with cancer, and her experience of God's love was a great gift. "It's so wonderful," she said, "the protective coating I had around my heart so I wouldn't be hurt anymore fell away. Every time I think about how much I'm loved by God, I just want to cry." Such love will melt any skeptic's heart.

If you are out on a limb with a need you can't handle, facing circumstances for which you have no solution, take a step of faith. If you're out on a limb, come down from the tree. Give the Lord a chance to come over. No matter what the hurt, disappointment, guilt, or skepticism Jesus is real. Our state of mind doesn't change that. God longs for fellowship with us. And I hope you'll welcome him gladly just like Zacchaeus welcomed him.

Questions for Reflection

1. When have you, or someone for whom you cared, felt like you were out on a limb or distant from God?

2. Was it (or is it) related to difficult circumstances, guilt, or skepticism?

3. What would it mean for you, or for someone you love, to "come down from the tree" and let Jesus "come over"? What would allowing your heart to be Jesus' home involve?

4. What do you see as the essential difference between hearing about God's love for you in Jesus Christ and experiencing it first-hand?

Dear Jesus, you came so that I wouldn't stay distant from you. You came so that you would be real to me, warm, accessible, and available. Help me in my weakness to come down from any distant perch I may be on that keeps me from intimacy with you. Give me the ability to make my heart your home and allow you to "help yourself" to my life. In Jesus' name, I pray. Amen.

Chapter 8

Seeing Jesus in the Master Fiddler

"A Reflection on Hebrews 2"

Introduction

Hebrews 2 tells us who Jesus is. He is high priest, exalted Lord, but also God in the flesh. Because these concepts are hard for us to understand and wrap our minds around, I am going to tell you a story I wrote that I think expresses something of what Hebrews 2 is trying to tell us about the nature and person of Jesus Christ. I borrowed the general idea from Walter Wangerin's story "The Ragman."[1]

Story

Have you seen the Master Fiddler? Tell me if you have. He's around here somewhere, and he's really good at making music.

He walks the streets and plays a certain tune, singing words to it that at first I didn't believe.

He sings out, "New fiddles in place of old." And people come from miles around, partly just to see him, and to hear his music. The notes he plays are clear as crystal, and sometimes people end up dancing in the streets. (Even though many of them who come to see him do not consider themselves the dancing sort.)

People come, bringing their splintered, warped, and shattered fiddles. But he never turns anyone away. In fact, the fiddler acts as if he knows them all. And folks have said that when he meets them, he will often play their favorite melody for a line or two before taking their own broken fiddle, putting it in a bag he carries on his back, and replacing it with a new one. It doesn't seem to matter to the Master Fiddler how dilapidated the instruments are that they give him. It doesn't matter if they are cracked or broken or have strings popping off.

He carries in his bag the broken fiddles that have grown silent. He carries the bag on his back, and it is from that same bag that he doles out new ones. They are made of wood that gleams amber in the sun. Folks say that those new fiddles almost play themselves, although they must first put the bow to the strings. People who thought they could never play before are playing now. Melodies as bubbly as a mountain stream are filling village streets and causing even dour residents to smile a little these days. No one understands why he doesn't run out of instruments. And where does he get those new fiddles? No one has a clue. The bag he carries is big and heavy. Folks have tried to lift it themselves, but only the Master Fiddler seems able to carry it. He alone carries all that splintered wood, those broken strings, and that silent music.

I saw a funny thing the other day. Funny, but bewildering at the same time. Someone came to the Master Fiddler but didn't want to give up his old fiddle. He told the Master Fiddler he didn't think his fiddle was all that bad. True, it couldn't make a sound, but that was life. The Master Fiddler just looked at him with eyes that flashed recognition. He obviously had seen this sort of thing before. "Let me give you something better," I heard him whisper eagerly. "Let me take the old and give you a new one that can play notes that will sound as clear as crystal, music as buoyant and resonant as a rushing brook that is filled to capacity in spring."

But the man backed away, clutching his old instrument. It had water stains all over it and the neck was bent forward. He told the Master Fiddler that he could repair it by himself. I saw him later with furniture polish and tape trying to fix his fiddle on his own. One day he'll go back to the Master Fiddler. Of course, he'll have to admit that his own fiddle is a lost cause. Maybe he'll go back when he realizes that the new fiddle is a free gift from the Master Fiddler and that he doesn't have to try so hard. Maybe he'll go back to the Master Fiddler when the tape falls off his old fiddle and the neck finally cracks in two.

It's strange how people cling to something that is so much less than what they could have. Like the woman who came by later on that day. I was standing near and saw it all. The Master Fiddler reached out his hand expectantly to take her old fiddle. It had no strings and was severely warped. "It belonged to my grandmother," she prattled. "She used to play it for me when I was very young. It turned my nightmares into dreams full of song. But I've neglected this old fiddle, and now look at it. It's worthless. But this needs to look respectable before I give it to you," she chirped and strode away. "Needs some strings at least and a good dusting off." "Wait!" cried the Master Fiddler and ran a few steps after her. "Instruments

71

that used to play but have now grown silent are my specialty. They do not put me off. Please, let me help you. Let me give you something new!" But she didn't even turn around. She was already far away, muttering something to herself about getting new strings and a pitch pipe. Her stride was determined, and she kicked up a lot of dust in her wake. I hope she'll come back to the Master Fiddler one day, after she's strung her fiddle with strings. Maybe then she'll realize that her fiddle still won't play right and the Master Fiddler will take broken instruments just as they are.

But have you seen the Master Fiddler anywhere? I know he's here, somewhere, and I really need him today. You see, my fiddle, it was playing a rather strident tune for a while. The strings were uncommonly tight, and when I tried to loosen them they wouldn't budge. Each time I raised the bow to play, the sound grew worse, until it screeched so badly I had to cover my ears. It all started when I lost the bow the Master Fiddler had given me. In a careless moment I misplaced that all-important bow. I looked everywhere for it, but finally had to go and buy a cheaper model at the store. This bow was said to work better when more pressure was applied to the strings. So that is what I tried to do—apply more pressure. Press down harder. The contrast was amazing because the bow the Master Fiddler had given to me was light and barely needed to touch the trembling surface of the strings before all manner of effusive melodies came lilting and cascading through the air. But this cheap bow with its heavy wood and need for pressure only emitted dull squawks and sometimes a piercing shriek. It was then that I knew the music was gone. I couldn't play anymore, and my days grew long and silent.

I went looking for him, the Master Fiddler. The empty silence grew more intense and piercing as day after day of searching drew me further and further from home, with no sign of him. I walked through villages and down winding lanes. I longed to see him, and at every bend in the road I thought perhaps he'd be there. But at every bend, I was disappointed. I asked folks if they had seen him. Some said yes, some said no. Some tried to sell me new bows and fiddles. But I'd had enough of counterfeit music. There was only one who could give me the melodic cadences I longed for. One night, the empty silence was deafening. My legs were sore, my heart was hurting in my chest, and I could go on no longer. I sat down on a rock and put my head in my hands.

And then he was there—the Master Fiddler, I mean. His hand was on my head, and as I looked up, I saw his eyes alive with wisdom. He reached into his bag and drew out a bow, exactly like the one he had given me before. It gleamed amber, even in the evening light, and the pale horsehair strung across it looked like gold cornsilk. I didn't even have to ask him for that bow. He knew I needed it. As he took the old bow from me, I placed the new bow on the strings, as lightly as a moth lands on a flower petal. Immediately music filled the air, tumbling out from my fiddle like an overzealous waterfall. Soon I was up and following him as together we played a melody that I seemed to have known long ago but had forgotten. His music lured me in exactly the right direction, for in moments we were at the front door of my home.

I must have slept and then awoke in the morning light. But he was gone, and I didn't get a chance to thank him. I don't know where I'd be if he hadn't shown up, put that new bow in my hand, and led me home again. That's the way the Master Fiddler is. He always wants you to have music. All you have to do is give up the old and exchange it for the new. And I'm smart enough to know that I can't fix the old on my own.

That's why I'm looking for the Master Fiddler today. I really need to thank him, and I can't stay here much longer. I have to find him because he's the only one I know who gives something new for free in place of the old. And I'm so grateful.

I should really let you know something more about the Master Fiddler before I go, though. It's kind of a secret, but if you really think about it, it makes sense. You see, the Master Fiddler is really more than what he appears to be. He had to limit himself in an enormous way so that we could catch on to this whole "old for new" idea. But we didn't get it for a long, long time. Who God was, I mean. Did I mention that the Master Fiddler is divine? (Hebrews 2:9: "We do see Jesus ... crowned with glory and honor.") It's hard to keep the two ideas going at once—human and divine, but they're both there in the Master Fiddler. Some people say that it's not possible to encapsulate a divine, eternal being into the fragility of human flesh. But I say to them, your thinking about God needs to get even bigger! God is big enough to do whatever God darn well pleases.

God knew we needed someone with a face like ours so we could understand. We needed God to climb down into our little tiny frame of reference, fenced in by space and time. So that's what God did—God became exactly like us. God in Jesus had toenails to clip and teeth to brush. He had whiskers and earlobes and had to blow his nose. And as he was, Jesus played a new song, a melody that brought heaven to earth in the simplest of ways. It amazes me that God chose to come and be like us, to enter a world of human limitations and fragility, to become subject to pain and suffering and death.

He experienced all of it—all the dross of life. He wept and

cried and suffered and mourned. He prayed, pleaded, dripped sweat, and bled and died in this world in which our music plays its bitter notes of death for every life. And then he came back. Yes, you heard what I said. He came back with a melody, far more clear and poignant than it had ever been before, far more powerful in its rhythm and its tone. And that resurrection music stayed with me.

Have you seen him? Have you see the Master Fiddler with the bag upon his back? He's around here somewhere. I'll let you know when I find him. But he will usually be found in the most unexpected places. You see, he's not concerned at all about appearances or flaunting his importance or sticking to the status quo. When folks are concerned with these things, it's bred from insecurity. No, the Master Fiddler is secure. He's been around a long time—from the beginning of time, in fact. In the very beginning he spoke and created time. (Hebrews 2:8: "God left nothing that is not subject to him.")

The Master Fiddler comes from an entirely different place. Things are much better there than they are here. There are no more broken strings and splintered wood, no empty silences or lives that have no melody. Where he comes from, why, the whole place is alive with a symphony. The entire population is constantly in song! This is the place where he actually wants us to go after this life is over. I can't wait to play my fiddle there. He's already asked me if I would, and I said yes!

You know, all I want to do is be best friends with the Master Fiddler. It's strange, but the Master Fiddler's melody is alive in me, and I can't stop thinking about him. I can't stop thinking about where I would be if he hadn't put that bow in my hands and led me home. I'd be dead if it weren't for the Master Fiddler and his melody. I can't stop thinking about the way he's willing to take my old instrument that doesn't play and give me music again.

I can't stop thinking about the Master Fiddler.

Reflection

Now this is simply a story that I wrote. But the Master Fiddler is a real person—Jesus Christ. You may not have recognized Jesus in the story of the Master Fiddler, but I hope you did. But even if you didn't, he sees *you* right now and is ready to take whatever *you* have to bring him. No matter what the difficulty, the heartache, or the burden, he will bear it for you. He will forgive you and give you a new start—no matter how far you've fallen.

This is the message of Hebrews 2. This is the nature of the awesome God we worship and belong to.

It often takes a lot of courage to bring our broken instruments, our broken and out-of-tune lives, to Jesus. By all appearances, most of us certainly don't look as though our lives are broken. We're very good at convincing ourselves and others everything is just fine, thank you. We give the illusion that our everything is in tune, that we are competent musicians. But inside, we often feel broken and discordant. We keep playing the wrong notes and just can't seem to get the rhythms right. Our need may not be physical so much as it is spiritual. We may be playing

- fragments of tunes that are the remnants of unfulfilled dreams and disappointed hopes;
- strident tunes that come from anxiety, pressure, and busyness;
- several discordant tunes simultaneously, all at different pitches.

This unharmonious discord, which can come from doing many things that have no significance, keeps us from hearing the melody of God's essential purpose and call for us and from making it a priority for our lives;

- cacophonous noises that shriek out the most difficult tune of all, and that's the tune of our own mortality. There's no escaping that one.

But Hebrews 2 cries out to us—there is a Savior. There is a Friend. There is a Brother. There is a merciful High Priest. There is one who came—it cost him everything—and made a way through the cross to resurrection to bring us the living music we need; to bring healing and hope, purpose and depth, cleansing and fulfillment to our otherwise shallow existence; to bring us eternal life, and free us from the fear of death. Why would our God do that for us? It is summed up in the words to a favorite melody we sing, "O the Deep, Deep Love of Jesus":

O the deep, deep love of Jesus, Vast, unmeasured, boundless free!
Rolling onward, leading homeward, to my glorious rest above.

Underneath me, all around me is the current of His love;
Leading onward, leading homeward to my glorious rest above.

O the deep, deep love of Jesus, Love of every love the best;
'Tis an ocean vast of blessing, 'tis the source of peace and rest.

O the deep, deep love of Jesus, 'Tis a heaven of heavens to me;
And it lifts me up to glory, for it lifts me up to Thee.

O the deep, deep love of Jesus, spread His praise from shore to
shore;
Sing of His greatness, sing of His goodness, sing of His love for
evermore.[2]

Questions for Reflection

1. What sort of fiddle are you playing? What kind of tunes does
the fiddle emit?

2. Jesus doesn't simply take your old instrument, but he gives
you a new one. What does that mean for you?

3. When have you needed the Lord to give you a new melody to
play? Did he do it? How?

4. In what ways can you celebrate the love of Jesus for you today?

*Lord, you are the maker of all that brings true joy. Thank you for giving
me a new song to play that praises your name and gives life to the world.
Help me not cling to old melodies and rhythms that are destructive, but let
go and allow you to play your life-giving cadences on the strings of my
heart. In Jesus' name, I pray. Amen.*

Chapter 9
Seeing Jesus in Suffering

Matthew 27:46; Mark 15:34; 1 Peter 2:24

When my daughter was six years old, she came into the kitchen with a tiny piece of trash in her hand one morning. She put it in the garbage and looked up at me. "Mommy," she said, "I'm going to clean up the world today."

I looked at her and remembered thinking in my early years of ministry that I would do the same. "I wish you would clean up the world," I told her. "I really wish you would." Even my six-year-old sensed that something is not quite right with the world.

Jesus was crucified, but the cross was not simply a means of execution. There are far simpler and easier ways to kill someone. Rather, crucifixion was really meant to be a means of torture. It was meant to "break the spirit" of the victim and create a horrific display for all who passed by. The message to onlookers was that Roman authority was not to be taken lightly. People lived in fear that at the whim of those in power such a thing could happen to them.

As if crucifixion were not bad enough, the flogging Jesus

endured beforehand was sufficient to kill someone in and of itself. The recent movie *The Passion of the Christ* depicted this in agonizing detail. We know that Jesus was sleep deprived, tormented, slapped, mocked, and given a crown of thorns, in addition to being flogged. No wonder he fell under the weight of the cross as he carried it up the hill.

It's hard to conceive of such brutality. Today, crosses are pretty, ornamental things, adorning church sanctuaries and hanging from ears, noses, and throats. Everyone, whether Christian or not, wears them it seems. I'm the first one to say to someone, "I like your cross. It's very pretty." But in Roman times, wearing a cross would have been a terribly perverse thing to do. It would have been like wearing a guillotine or an electric chair around your neck.

Unpleasant as contemplating the crucifixion is, don't slap the resurrection on the face of the cross just yet or rush by it too fast. There is something valuable and good to be found amid the suffering in this instrument of torture.

In the crude splintered face of the cross, God is present with us. God is with us in our pain.

Even in the midst of the worst the world has to offer, in the depths and the muck of life, and when we are at our lowest, God is there. The pain on Jesus' face as he hung on the cross tells us that God not only knows about our pain—as you would know something by reading it in a book—but also feels our pain. God in Christ chose to experience our loneliness, our fear, our despair, and also the effects of our sin, injustice, betrayal, and hatred. "My God, my God, why have you forsaken me?" cries Jesus from this brutal cross—the only time he ever refers to God this way. Usually

Jesus calls God "Daddy" or "Father," but when he was on the cross, Jesus felt distant from God just as God seems distant to many who are hurting today. And being distant and separated from God is ultimately the greatest pain.

If someone says he or she is in pain, I respond by rushing in to try to fix it, to take away whatever horrible thing is causing pain. This, in some ways, is the right response; a response of compassion to relieve suffering. Yet, God didn't do that where we were concerned. Instead of simply fixing the problem by getting rid of our sin and our pain, God chose instead to become human and to experience sin and pain. Even worse than the physical pain Jesus experienced was the alienation from God—the weight of human sin and pain he bore separated him from God, and this was the worst torment. Yet, the cross tells us that no matter what our pain, God has been there and has conquered it all.

I had the opportunity to meet a woman who had been a prisoner of war. She had strong lines in her face and a light in her eye. She had been the victim of torture. "I never realized," she told me, "that there was a place I could go inside of me, where Christ was, that my tormenters could never take away from me. That place was at the center of my being and very quiet. I go there often, even today." No matter how deep the pain, God's love and presence are deeper still.

We miss something life changing when we stop listening to what pain can teach us. Sometimes pain can be instructive and helpful. That's why it is good to be able to look at the cross although it goes against our grain. Today we have more painkillers than ever before. There seems to be a remedy for nearly every kind of pain. As a mother of three, I use child-strength ibuprofen regularly. It is truly amazing and quickly causes all of the symptoms to disappear!

Because they don't feel sick anymore, my children start running about the house, which sometimes ends up making them sicker. The body's messages of pain serve to alert us that something is wrong and that we need to rest.

God's pain in Jesus Christ serves to help us recognize our broken condition and give us a vision of who we were meant to be.

In the contorted face of our crucified Lord, we recognize our own brokenness and the pain that this separation from God has brought into our lives. We call it sin, and sin means "missing the mark." By our sin, we miss living the life we were *meant* to live. We were made for intimacy with God. Just as an eagle was made to soar freely though the sky rather than be bound captive in a cage at the zoo, so also we were not made to exist apart from a dynamic life-giving, soaring relationship with our Creator. And yet it's what we chose way back when, in the Garden of Eden, we mistrusted God's good intent for us and decided to do it on our own.

Ever since then, we've known pain, and it has made life hard. Sometimes very hard! On the cross, Christ mirrors to us the brokenness and separation from God caused by our sin. Our focus on self and attempting to control our own lives keep us from intimate communion with the One who truly loves us and completes us. We all have a space inside us that is shaped just for God—a God-shaped vacuum—that we try to fill up with substitutes. But substitutes never really work. Just like substitute teachers never taught us what we really needed to know; and though margarine tastes like butter, it tends to burn when you try to cook with it. Addictions burn us, too, and take on all forms from alcoholism to being driven to succeed. The only way to have our bondage to these substitutions broken, and our longings fulfilled, is to be in relationship with our Creator. It's the way it was meant to be. We are genetically predisposed to living in fellowship with God.

"People who come to church have such perfect, happy lives!" someone said to me a while ago. "They're always smiling and happy in their nice clothes, and I sit there feeling miserable and out of touch. I just can't go to church anymore." I've been in the ministry now for eighteen years and know that people do not have the perfect, happy lives that appearances might suggest. I know that there's a whole lot more pain out there than meets the eye. The substitutes haven't worked, and we long for something more.

We all need a Savior, no matter how successful we may appear on the surface. The God of Jesus Christ is for all of us who have come to our senses like the prodigal son and know we need forgiveness and the divine love of our Creator to fill us in all the empty parts that cry out to be filled.

The cross reminds us that we belong to a pursuing God.

The extent to which God will go to find us, forgive us, and draw us in beyond our human abilities to understand. If it takes becoming human and suffering on a cross and bearing the whole tangled mass of the world's sins in order to right what is wrong with our spiritual state, then God will do that. What we might call "the plan of salvation" really points to the amazing concept that God wants our company, desires to be in relationship with us, and pursues us in love—going far beyond what any of us might think "reasonable." The classic poem "The Hound of Heaven"[1] compares God in just this way, as a hound that never ceases chasing its prey.

SEEING JESUS

Our suffering, in the hands of the living God, is moldable, bendable, and usable.

God, in Jesus Christ, can transform our pain into something usable for glory. Jesus used ordinary dirt and spit to make the blind man see again. The cross, once an instrument of torture, became a symbol of victory for Christians all over the world. We can wear it around our necks as a reminder that God transformed the worst symbol of pain—a foolish symbol, a weak, barbarous symbol—to a universal symbol of healing, forgiveness, and restoration. In the hands of God, the very stuff of pain can be used to change the world.

I can only say this because God has used the dirt and spit of my own life to bring sight to my eyes. I am an introvert. I consistently come up that way on all the personality tests I have ever taken. It surprises people, and it surprises me that I have been called to a profession in which I am constantly with people, talking to them, walking with them, praying with them, standing up in front of them preaching. When I was little, I was so shy that if the doorbell rang, I ran and hid. My shyness continued through my preteen years. I never said a word in the classroom. I remember so clearly knowing the right answer one day in class, when no one else did, and trying my darndest to raise my hand. My heart pounded furiously in my chest, and I felt weak and shaky. But I couldn't get my hand up before the teacher told us the answer. Well, you can imagine how this isolated me from others and how lonely I became. At twelve years old, I had had just about enough. I was sitting on the couch one afternoon, crying, just crying. The radio was on softly, and then "Amazing Grace" was played. It was the first time I had ever been flooded with the presence of God. I stayed awake all night reading scripture. And I knew I could be alone as long as I was loved. And with God at my side, I was never alone.

Gradually, the Lord has shown me, through training, therapy, and supervision, that what I had actually perceived as a weakness could be used as a strength. My tendency to look inward has helped me in pastoral counseling situations in which knowing one's own dynamics is helpful in assisting others to discern theirs. So the dirt and the spit of my life have become redemptive in this way.

Remember that the risen Christ in his glorified body still bears the wounds of the cross in his hands and feet. But those wounds heal us today, and it is through them that resurrection life flows out to us. The Bible is not a Disney story or a fairy tale. Otherwise, we would just erase those wounds from the risen Christ and make everyone live happily ever after. That would certainly be a much nicer story. But we're not talking about a fantasy. God isn't interested in starring in a Disney flick. Rather, God chooses to be involved in our lives— in the reality of human life that includes pain and heartbreak and disappointment and selfishness and sin. Real life leaves its scars, and real life means pain, especially when you live it in love. And yet, God confronts us in Jesus Christ, holds out his scarred hands, and says, "Walk with me along this path of woundedness." And in the hands of God our wounds, too, can bring healing to a broken world.

Questions for Reflection

1. What has the pain in your life taught you? Has it been helpful or instructive?

2. How does looking at the cross help you when you are in pain? What does the cross say to the world, to the church, and to each person about pain?

3. Have you ever felt that God was pursuing you, even in the midst of your pain?

4. Does knowing that Jesus suffered for you make a difference when you are suffering?

5. When have you been able to use your suffering to empathize with another? When have you been, as Henri Nouwen terms it, a "Wounded Healer"?[2]

6. The problem of pain and evil in the world has been debated for centuries. Some theologians have said that in this world we live between the "already" of Christ's victory over death and the forgiveness of our sins, and the "not yet" of still living in a broken world. What are your thoughts about God's role in suffering? Does God cause pain and suffering? Does God simply use them and work transformation through them? What is God's future plan? (See Revelation 21:1-5.)

Jesus, you are Lord of all suffering and more victorious than the worst that evil can do. Help us in the midst of our broken world to remember this and be secure in the reality that when the worst difficulties arise, you will never leave us or forsake us, that indeed resurrection emerges over and over again from the depth of our pain when we trust you with the outcome. Help us trust, to live with confidence in your love, so that you can become a conduit of amazing grace to us. In Jesus' name, I pray. Amen.

Notes

1. Seeing Jesus by Expanding Your Context

1. Dr. Seuss, *The Cat in the Hat* (New York: Random House, 1957); Dr. Seuss, *Horton Hears a Who* (New York: Random House, 1954); Dr. Seuss, *Green Eggs and Ham* (New York: Random House, 1960).

2. Dr. Seuss, *On Beyond Zebra* (New York: Random House, 1955).

2. Seeing Jesus by Letting Go of What We Cling To

1. Prayer of Saint Francis of Assisi.

2. CALFED (bought out by Citibank).

3. From the Nobel eMuseum website: http://www.nobel.se/peace/laureates/1980/esquivel-acceptance.html.

4. Mother Teresa.

4. Seeing Jesus When He Seems Far Away

1. The idea for my personal illustration about the mountain came from James S. Stewart's sermon "Beyond Disillusionment to Faith" in *Best Sermons,* ed. Paul Butler (New York: Van Nostrand Co., 1962), vol. 3.

2. Hugh T. Kerr and John M. Mulder, eds. *Conversions: The Christian Experience* (Grand Rapids: Eerdmans, 1983), 37.

3. Brennan Manning, *The Signature of Jesus,* rev. ed. (Sisters, Ore.: Multnomah, 1996).

5. Seeing Jesus in the Storms

1. This ancient proverb appears in the literature of a number of cultures, and was also recorded in the 1736 edition of Benjamin Franklin's *Poor Richard's Almanac.*

7. Seeing Jesus When You Are "Out on a Limb"

1. Anne Lamott, *Traveling Mercies: Some Thoughts on Faith* (New York: Anchor Books, 1999), 49-50.

8. Seeing Jesus in the Master Fiddler

1. Walter Wangerin, *Ragman and Other Cries of Faith* (San Francisco: Harper & Row, 1984).

2. "O the Deep, Deep Love of Jesus" in *The Hymnal for Worship and Celebration* (Waco, Tex.: Word Music, 1996), 211.

9. Seeing Jesus in Suffering

1. Francis Thompson, "The Hound of Heaven."

2. Henri J. M. Nouwen, *The Wounded Healer: Ministry in Contemporary Society* (Garden City, N. Y.: Doubleday, 1972).